MW01012868

Specimen
Aural Tests

from 2011

Grades 4 & 5

ABRSM

Introduction

Minor modifications to some aural tests took effect for ABRSM Practical graded music exams from January 2011 (all subjects except Jazz). For further details of the changes visit www.abrsm.org/aural. This book of specimen tests provides practice examples which demonstrate the style and difficulty level of the tests at Grades 4 and 5.

Listening lies at the heart of all good music-making. Developing aural awareness is fundamental to musical training because having a 'musical ear' impacts on all aspects of musicianship. By integrating aural activities in imaginative ways throughout the lesson, preparation for the aural tests within an exam will be a natural extension of what is already an essential part of the learning experience.

Using the specimen tests

When preparing for an exam, these specimen tests will provide valuable practice material to help prepare candidates for what to expect on the day. Guided by the examples provided, teachers will also be able to devise their own exercises, ideally using music their students are currently working on.

What does each test involve?

A description of the tasks involved in each test, as well as any relevant parameters, is given in the left-hand column at the start of each set of tests. The same information can also be found in the syllabus booklet.

What will happen in the exam?

The examiner will deliver each test following a set of spoken words and instructions (referred to as the 'rubric'). All music extracts will be played on the piano, and the examiner will be ready to prompt the candidate if necessary where there is hesitation. In this book, the examiner rubric is printed in the right-hand column at the start of each set of tests and at the top of any subsequent pages, so that teachers are able to deliver the tests to their students in a way that mirrors the exam experience.

For any test that requires a sung response, it is pitch rather than vocal quality that is being assessed. The examiner will be happy to adapt to the vocal range of the candidate, whose responses may be sung to any vowel (or consonant followed by vowel), or hummed or whistled (and at a different octave, if appropriate).

Where tests require a spoken response, candidates are encouraged to use Italian terms where appropriate, but there will be no disadvantage to those who do not, provided that their response is equally clear and accurate.

Insert for Test B

A separate insert is provided for the student to use for Tests 4B and 5B.

Mock tests

A mock test for each grade (a set of recorded tests presented in order, as they would be in the exam) is available as a free audio download from the ABRSM website: www.abrsm.org/mockauraltests. The relevant tests are marked in the book with the following symbol MOCK TEST .

Answers

Model answers for Tests 4C(i) and 5C(i) are printed at the back of this book, as a guide to the sort of responses that would be successful in the exam. In some cases there are other ways of responding that would be equally successful, so the answers should be used only as a guide. It should also be noted that in an exam the examiner will not provide answers.

How are the aural tests marked?

The mark for aural tests is arrived at by making an overall assessment of the candidate's performance during the set of tests as a whole, and relating this to the assessment criteria shown below. Rather than starting at zero and awarding marks as the tests proceed, or at 18 and then deducting marks, examiners use the principle of marking positively or negatively from the pass mark. The mark then reflects the cumulative balance of strengths and weaknesses that the candidate has demonstrated, taking into account the accuracy, perceptiveness and quality of the responses given.

Assessment criteria (all grades)

Distinction

(18) • Quick, accurate and perceptive responses

Merit

(15–17) • Good responses

• Minor errors or hesitation

Pass

(12–14) • Approximately half the tests correctly answered

• Evidence of awareness, despite hesitation and error

Below Pass

(9–11) • Slow and uncertain responses

• Inaccuracy in parts of all tests

(6–8) • Very slow and mostly incorrect responses

• All tests entirely inaccurate

(0) • No work offered

Access (for candidates with specific needs)

Deaf or hearing-impaired candidates may opt to respond to alternative tests in place of the standard tests, if requested at the time of entry. The syllabus for these tests is available free on request from ABRSM. For blind or partially-sighted candidates, alternative tests are available for Test B. For further information about alternative tests and access for candidates with specific needs please contact ABRSM's Access Co-ordinator or visit the website.

Telephone +44 (0)20 7636 5400

Textphone +44 (0)20 7637 2582

Email accesscoordinator@abrsm.ac.uk

www.abrsm.org/specialneeds

Other aural training resources from ABRSM

For further examples and comprehensive advice on preparing candidates for aural tests, teachers are referred to the new edition of *Aural Training in Practice* (2011).

Please note that the music extracts in this book have been freely adapted where necessary for the purpose of the aural tests.

First published in 2010 by ABRSM (Publishing) Ltd, a wholly owned subsidiary of ABRSM, 24 Portland Place, London W1B 1LU, United Kingdom

Reprinted in 2010, 2011

© 2010 by The Associated Board of the Royal Schools of Music

Cover and text design by Vermillion

Music and text origination by Andrew Jones

Additional text setting by Hope Services Ltd

Printed in England by Halstan & Co. Ltd, Amersham, Bucks.

To sing or play from memory a melody played twice by the examiner. The melody will be within the range of an octave, in a major or minor key with up to three sharps or flats. First the examiner will play the key-chord and the starting note and then count in two bars. (If the candidate chooses to play, the examiner will also name the key-chord and the starting note, as appropriate for the instrument.) If necessary, the examiner will play the melody again and allow a second attempt (although this will affect the assessment).

*Here is a melody for you to repeat. Would you prefer to sing it or play it? * ... I'll play it twice. Here is the key-chord* [play] *and your starting note* [play]. [Count in two bars, then play the melody once.] *Here it is again.* [Repeat the melody without counting in.] *... Thank you.*

* [If the candidate chooses to play, name as well as play the key-chord and starting note. With transposing instruments use only the examples specified, naming the key-chord and starting note as shown, according to the instrument.]

1 Allegretto — Gedike

© Copyright Anglo-Soviet Music Press
Reproduced by permission of Boosey & Hawkes Music Publishers Ltd

2 Minuet — Lully

3 Moderato — Spanish carol

4 Moderato — G. Jacob

© Copyright 1934 by Gordon Jacob
Exclusively licensed to J. Curwen & Sons Limited.
All rights transferred to G. Schirmer Limited.
All rights reserved. International Copyright Secured.
Used by permission of G. Schirmer Limited.

5 Sostenuto (Andantino) — Hérold

Moderato — J. S. Bach

Moderato — Byrd

Moderato — Anon.

Transposing instruments
in B♭: G major, starting note B; **in F**: C major, starting note E; **in E♭**: D major, starting note F♯

Con moto — Grieg

Transposing instruments
in B♭: E minor, starting note B; **in F**: A minor, starting note E; **in E♭**: B minor, starting note F♯

Adagio — Haydn

Transposing instruments
in B♭: G major, starting note D; **in F**: C major, starting note G; **in E♭**: D major, starting note A

To sing five notes from score in free time. The candidate may choose to sing from treble or bass clef. The notes will be within the range of a third above and below the tonic in the key of C, F or G major. The test will begin and end on the tonic and will not contain intervals greater than a third. First the examiner will name and play the key-chord and the starting note. If necessary, the examiner will help the candidate by playing and identifying the correct note if any note is sung at the wrong pitch.

[When appropriate: *Would you prefer to sing notes in treble clef or bass clef?*]
Please sing the notes at number ... on this page.
Sing them slowly, and I'll help by giving you the right note if you sing a wrong one. Here is the key-chord [name and play] *and this is your starting note* [name and play]. *... Thank you.*

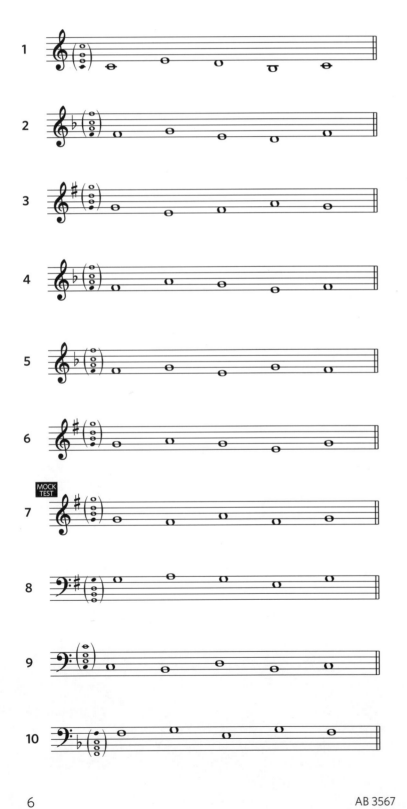

AB 3567

4B Grade 4

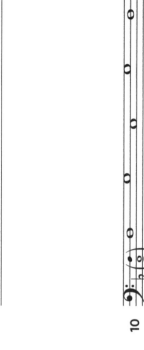

1

2

3

4

5

6

7

MOCK TEST

8

9

10

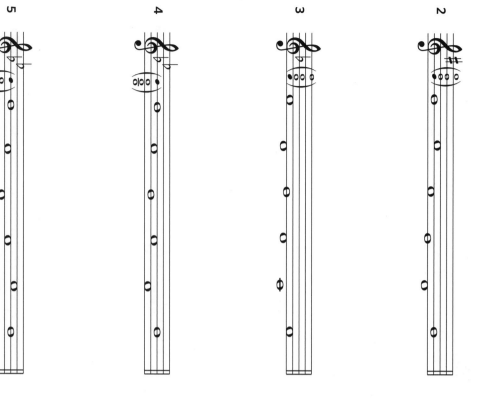
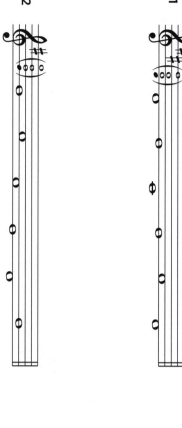
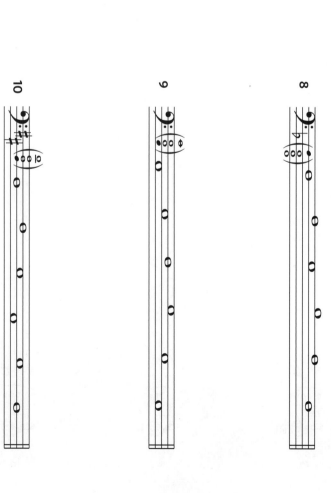
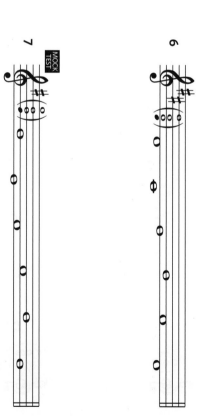

(i) **To answer questions about two features of a piece played by the examiner.** Before playing, the examiner will tell the candidate which two features the questions will be about. The first will be *one* of the following: dynamics, articulation, tempo, tonality; the second will be character.

(ii) **To clap the rhythm of the notes in an extract from the same piece, and to identify whether it is in two time, three time or four time.** The examiner will play the extract twice (unharmonized), after which the candidate should clap back the rhythm. The examiner will then ask whether the music is in two time, three time or four time. The candidate is *not* required to state the time signature.

(i) *Listen to this piece, then I'll ask you about ...* [choose one of the first three features listed below the piece] *and about character.* [After playing, ask one question at a time.]

(ii) *Now clap the rhythm of the notes in this phrase, after I've played it twice more.* [Play the extract once.] *Here it is again.* [Repeat the extract.] ... *Is it in two time, three time or four time? ... Thank you.*

E. German

1

© Copyright 1892 Novello & Company Limited for France, Italy, Mexico and Spain
All Rights Reserved.
Used by Permission.

Dynamics: *Describe the dynamics in this piece.*
Tempo: *Did the tempo change or did it always stay the same?*
Tonality: *Was the music in a major key or in a minor key?*
Character: *What in the music gives this piece its character?*

(i) *Listen to this piece, then I'll ask you about …*
[choose one of the first three features listed
below the piece] *and about character.*
[After playing, ask one question at a time.]

(ii) *Now clap the rhythm of the notes in this phrase,
after I've played it twice more.* [Play the extract
once.] *Here it is again.* [Repeat the extract.] …
Is it in two time, three time or four time? …
Thank you.

Reger

Dynamics: *Was the last change in dynamics sudden or gradual?*
Articulation: *Were the chords in the accompaniment mainly smooth or mainly detached?*
Tempo: *Was there any change in tempo, or did it always stay the same?*
Character: *What in the music gives this piece its character?*

AB 3567

Gurlitt

Dynamics: *Did the dynamic changes happen suddenly or gradually?*
Articulation: *Were the chords played with smooth or detached notes?*
Tonality: *Was the music in a major key or in a minor key?*
Character: *What gives this music its character?*

Sigurbjörnsson

Dynamics: *Describe the dynamics in this piece.*
Articulation: *Were the accompanying chords smooth or detached?*
Tonality: *Was the music in a major key or in a minor key?*
Character: *What in the music gives this piece its character?*

(i) *Listen to this piece, then I'll ask you about* ...
[choose one of the first three features listed
below the piece] *and about character.*
[After playing, ask one question at a time.]

(ii) *Now clap the rhythm of the notes in this phrase,*
after I've played it twice more. [Play the extract
once.] *Here it is again.* [Repeat the extract.] ...
Is it in two time, three time or four time? ...
Thank you.

Allegro moderato

Villa-Lobos

© Copyright 1948 (Renewed) by Music Sales Corporation
All Rights Reserved. International Copyright Secured.
Used by Permission.

Dynamics: *Describe the dynamics in this piece.*
Tempo: *Was there any change in tempo, or did it always stay the same?*
Tonality: *Did the music end in a major key or in a minor key?*
Character: *What gives this piece its musical character?*

AB 3567

Tempo di mazurka

Grechaninov

6

clap

molto rall.

a tempo

rall.

Articulation: *In the middle section of the piece, was the lower part smooth or detached?*

Tempo: *Was there any change in tempo, or did it always stay the same?*

Tonality: *Did the music end in a major key or in a minor key?*

Character: *What gives this piece its musical character?*

(i) *Listen to this piece, then I'll ask you about ...*
[choose one of the first three features listed
below the piece] *and about character.*
[After playing, ask one question at a time.]

(ii) *Now clap the rhythm of the notes in this phrase,
after I've played it twice more.* [Play the extract
once.] *Here it is again.* [Repeat the extract.] ...
Is it in two time, three time or four time? ...
Thank you.

Stephen Duro

Moderate jazz waltz

clap

© 1997 by The Associated Board of the Royal Schools of Music

Dynamics: *Describe the dynamics in the second half of this piece.*
Tempo: *Was there any change in tempo, or did it always stay the same?*
Tonality: *Was the music in a major key or in a minor key?*
Character: *What in the music gives this piece its character?*

AB 3567

Steibelt

Dynamics: *Describe the dynamics in the first half of the piece.*
Articulation: *Were the quiet phrases played with smooth or detached notes?*
Tonality: *Did the music end in a major key or in a minor key?*
Character: *What in the music gives this piece its character?*

Jensen

Dynamics: *The music began loudly. Describe the dynamic changes after that.*
Articulation: *What was the difference in articulation between the first and last phrases?*
Tonality: *Did the piece end in a major key or in a minor key?*
Character: *What gives this piece its musical character?*

(i) *Listen to this piece, then I'll ask you about ...*
[choose one of the first three features listed
below the piece] *and about character.*
[After playing, ask one question at a time.]

(ii) *Now clap the rhythm of the notes in this phrase,*
after I've played it twice more. [Play the extract
once.] *Here it is again.* [Repeat the extract.] *...*
Is it in two time, three time or four time? ...
Thank you.

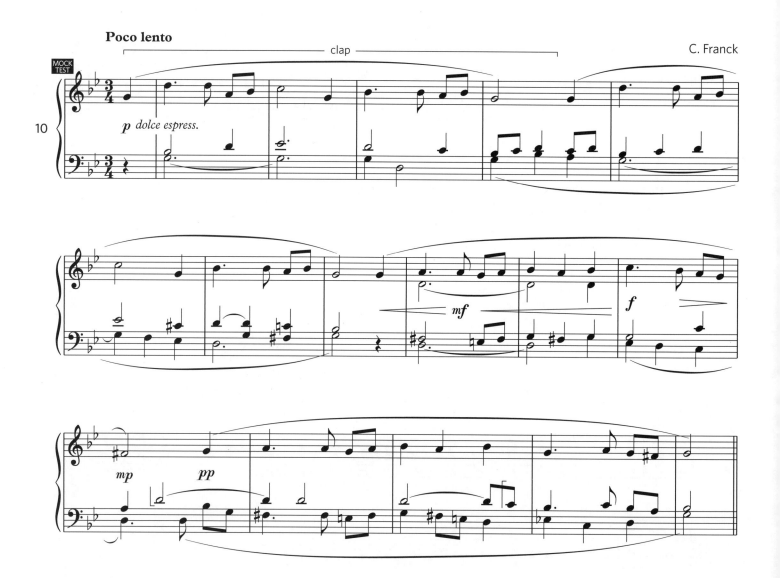

Dynamics: *Describe the dynamic changes in this piece.*
Tempo: *Was there any tempo change, or did it always stay the same?*
Tonality: *Did the music end in a major key or in a minor key?*
Character: *What in the music gives this piece its character?*

To sing or play from memory a melody played twice by the examiner. The melody will be within the range of an octave, in a major or minor key with up to three sharps or flats. First the examiner will play the key-chord and the starting note and then count in two bars. (If the candidate chooses to play, the examiner will also name the key-chord and the starting note, as appropriate for the instrument.) If necessary, the examiner will play the melody again and allow a second attempt (although this will affect the assessment).

Here is a melody for you to repeat. Would you prefer to sing it or play it? * *... I'll play it twice. Here is the key-chord* [play] *and your starting note* [play]**.** [Count in two bars, then play the melody once.] *Here it is again.* [Repeat the melody without counting in.] *... Thank you.*

* [If the candidate chooses to play, name as well as play the key-chord and starting note. With transposing instruments use only the examples specified, naming the key-chord and starting note as shown, according to the instrument.]

1

2

3

4

5

6

Here is a melody for you to repeat. Would you prefer to sing it or play it? * *... I'll play it twice. Here is the key-chord* [play] *and your starting note* [play]*.* [Count in two bars, then play the melody once.] *Here it is again.* [Repeat the melody without counting in.] *... Thank you.*

* [If the candidate chooses to play, name as well as play the key-chord and starting note. With transposing instruments use only the examples specified, naming the key-chord and starting note as shown, according to the instrument.]

7 MOCK TEST **Andante** Gluck

8 **Moderato** English folksong

Transposing instruments
in B♭: E minor, starting note G; **in F**: A minor, starting note C; **in E♭**: B minor, starting note D

9 **Andante** Welsh melody

Transposing instruments
in B♭: C major, starting note G; **in F**: F major, starting note C; **in E♭**: G major, starting note D

10 **Andante** Stamitz

Transposing instruments
in B♭: E minor, starting note B; **in F**: A minor, starting note E; **in E♭**: B minor, starting note F♯

To sing six notes from score in free time. The candidate may choose to sing from treble or bass clef. The notes will be within the range of a fifth above and a fourth below the tonic, in a major key with up to two sharps or flats. The test will begin and end on the tonic and will not contain intervals greater than a third, except for the rising fourth from dominant to tonic. First the examiner will name and play the key-chord and the starting note. If necessary, the examiner will help the candidate by playing and identifying the correct note if any note is sung at the wrong pitch.

[When appropriate: *Would you prefer to sing notes in treble clef or bass clef?*]
Please sing the notes at number ... on this page. Sing them slowly, and I'll help by giving you the right note if you sing a wrong one. Here is the key-chord [name and play] *and this is your starting note* [name and play]*. ... Thank you.*

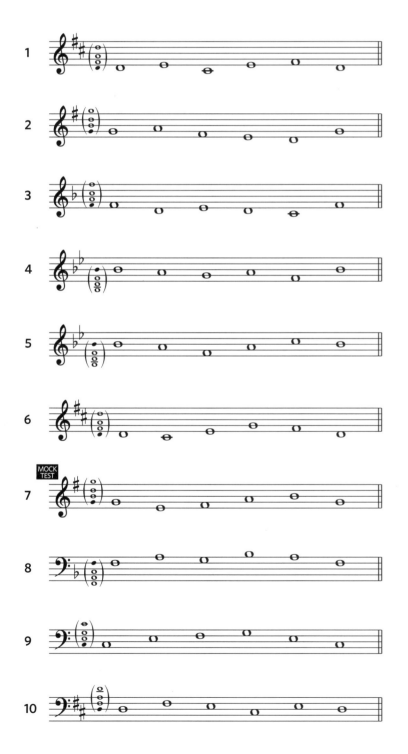

(i) **To answer questions about two features of a piece played by the examiner.** Before playing, the examiner will tell the candidate which two features the questions will be about. The first will be *one* of the following: dynamics, articulation, tempo, tonality, character; the second will be style and period.

(ii) **To clap the rhythm of the notes in an extract from the same piece, and to identify whether it is in two time, three time or four time.** The examiner will play the extract twice (unharmonized), after which the candidate should clap back the rhythm. The examiner will then ask whether the music is in two time, three time or four time. The candidate is *not* required to state the time signature.

(i) *Listen to this piece, then I'll ask you about …* [choose one of the first three features listed below the piece] *and about style and period.* [After playing, ask one question at a time.]

(ii) *Now clap the rhythm of the notes in this phrase, after I've played it twice more.* [Play the extract once.] *Here it is again.* [Repeat the extract.] … *Is it in two time, three time or four time?* … *Thank you.*

* Omit ornaments for clapping.

Articulation: ***Describe the articulation used in this piece.***
Tonality: ***Was this piece in a major key or in a minor key?***
Character: ***What in the music gives this piece its character?***
Style and Period: ***Is this Baroque, Romantic or 20th-century music? Which musical features tell you that?***

Gershwin

Largamente con moto [straight quavers]

Prelude II (Andante con moto e poco rubato)
Music by George Gershwin
© (Renewed) 1927 W B Music Corp, London, W6 8BS
Warner/Chappell North America Ltd
GERSHWIN® and GEORGE GERSHWIN® are registered trademarks of Gershwin Enterprises
Reproduced by permission of Faber Music Ltd
All Rights Reserved.

Dynamics: *Were the dynamic changes sudden or gradual? Where was the quietest point?*
Tempo: *Was there any tempo change, or did it always stay the same?*
Tonality: *Was the music in a major key or in a minor key?*
Style and Period: *Is this a Classical, Romantic or 20th-century piece? What in the music tells you that?*

(i) *Listen to this piece, then I'll ask you about ...*
[choose one of the first three features listed
below the piece] *and about style and period.*
[After playing, ask one question at a time.]

(ii) *Now clap the rhythm of the notes in this phrase,*
after I've played it twice more. [Play the extract
once.] *Here it is again.* [Repeat the extract.] ...
Is it in two time, three time or four time? ...
Thank you.

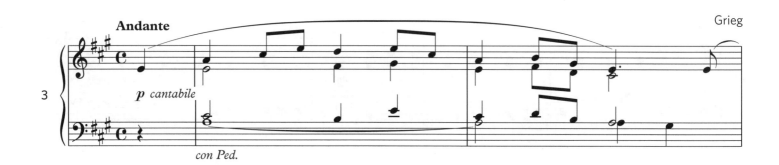

Grieg

* Omit grace notes and rall. for clapping.

Dynamics: *Describe the dynamics in this piece.*
Tempo: *Was there any change in tempo, or did it stay the same throughout?*
Character: *What in the music gives this piece its character?*
Style and Period: *Is the style and period of this music Baroque, Classical or Romantic?*
                 Which features of the music suggest that?

Rameau

* Omit ornament for clapping.

Dynamics: *Were the dynamic changes gradual or sudden? Where was the loudest point?*
Tempo: *Was there any change in tempo, or did it always stay the same?*
Tonality: *Did the music end in a major key or in a minor key?*
Style and Period: *Is the style and period of this music Baroque, Romantic or 20th century?*
Which features of the music suggest that?

(i) *Listen to this piece, then I'll ask you about …*
[choose one of the first three features listed
below the piece] *and about style and period.*
[After playing, ask one question at a time.]

(ii) *Now clap the rhythm of the notes in this phrase,
after I've played it twice more.* [Play the extract
once.] *Here it is again.* [Repeat the extract.] *…
Is it in two time, three time or four time? …
Thank you.*

Mozart

Dynamics: *What was the dynamic difference between the first and second phrases?*
Tempo: *Was there any tempo change, or did it always stay the same?*
Tonality: *Was the music in a major key or in a minor key?*
Style and Period: *Is this piece from the Baroque, Classical or Romantic period? What tells you this?*

© Copyright 1921. New Edition © Copyright 1999 for all countries Chester Music Limited, 14–15 Berners Street, London W1T 3LJ, United Kingdom.
Co-published for Spain and Spanish-speaking territories (and including Portugal but excluding Brazil) with Manuel de Falla Ediciones.
All Rights Reserved. Used by Permission.

Dynamics: *Describe the dynamics in this piece.*
Tempo: *Did the tempo change or did it always stay the same?*
Character: *What in the music gives this piece its character?*
Style and Period: *Is this a Baroque, Classical or 20th-century piece? Which musical features tell you that?*

(i) *Listen to this piece, then I'll ask you about ...*
[choose one of the first three features listed
below the piece] *and about style and period.*
[After playing, ask one question at a time.]

(ii) *Now clap the rhythm of the notes in this phrase,*
after I've played it twice more. [Play the extract
once.] *Here it is again.* [Repeat the extract.] ...
Is it in two time, three time or four time? ...
Thank you.

Christopher Norton

* Omit grace notes for clapping.

© Copyright 1990 by Boosey & Hawkes Music Publishers Ltd

Articulation: *Was the lower part played smoothly or with detached notes?*
Tonality: *Was this piece in a major key or in a minor key?*
Character: *What in the music gives this piece its character?*
Style and Period: *Is this a Classical, Romantic or 20th-century piece? Which musical features tell you that?*

AB 3567

Lutosławski

* Omit rit. for clapping.

© Copyright 1947 by Polskie Wydawnictwo Muzyczne – PWM Edition Kraków.
Copyright renewed 1975 by Polskie Wydawnictwo Muzyczne – PWM Edition.
Exclusively licensed in 1990 to Chester Music Limited, 14–15 Berners Street,
London W1T 3LJ, United Kingdom for the World excluding Poland, Albania,
Bulgaria, China, the Czech and Slovak Republics, Slovenia, Croatia,
Bosnia and Herzegovina, Montenegro, Serbia and Macedonia, Cuba,
North Korea, Vietnam, Rumania, Hungary and the former USSR.
All Rights Reserved. International Copyright Secured.
Used by Permission.

Dynamics: *Where was the loudest point in the music? And the quietest?*
Articulation: *Were the notes in the upper part mainly smooth or mainly detached?*
Tempo: *What happened to the tempo after the slower middle section?*
Style and Period: *Is this a Classical, Romantic or 20th-century piece? What in the music tells you that?*

(i) ***Listen to this piece, then I'll ask you about …*** [choose one of the first three features listed below the piece] ***and about style and period.*** [After playing, ask one question at a time.]

(ii) ***Now clap the rhythm of the notes in this phrase, after I've played it twice more.*** [Play the extract once.] ***Here it is again.*** [Repeat the extract.] … ***Is it in two time, three time or four time?*** … ***Thank you.***

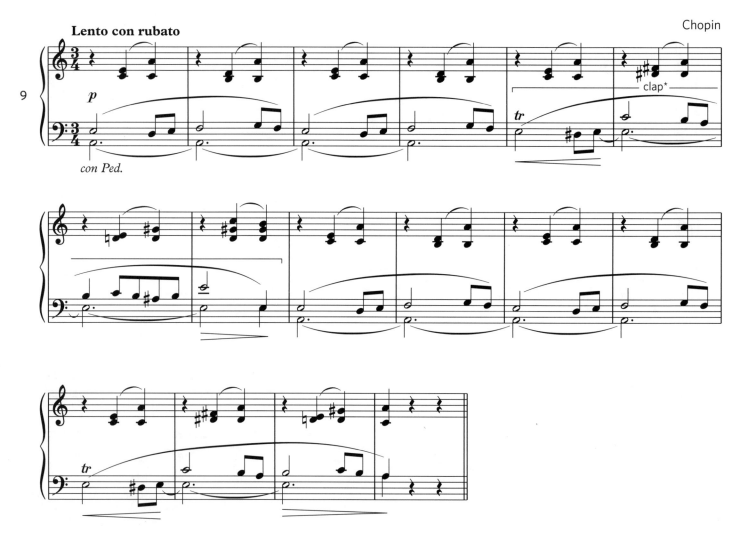

Chopin

Lento con rubato

con Ped.

* Play in strict time and omit trill for clapping.

Dynamics: ***What can you say about the dynamic level and dynamic changes in this piece?***
Articulation: ***Was the melody phrased smoothly or in a detached style?***
Character: ***What in the music gives this piece its character?***
Style and Period: ***Is this Baroque, Classical or Romantic music? Which features of the music suggest that?***

AB 3567

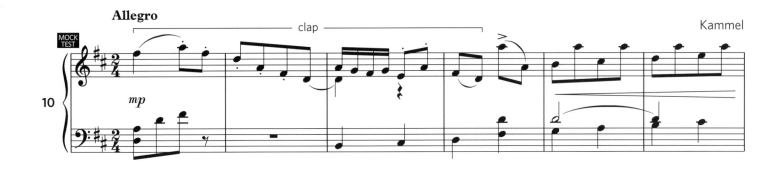

Dynamics: ***Was the end louder or quieter than the beginning? Was the dynamic at the end reached suddenly or gradually?***

Articulation: ***During the final phrase, was the articulation smooth or detached?***

Tempo: ***Did the tempo vary or did it stay the same?***

Style and Period: ***Is the style and period of this music Classical, Romantic or 20th century? Which features of the music suggest that?***

Answers

Model answers for Tests 4C(i) and 5C(i) are printed here as a guide to the sort of responses that would be successful in an exam. Full credit would be given to these answers, if given promptly and confidently. However, they are neither definitive nor comprehensive and there are other ways of responding to the questions that would be equally successful. For some questions, candidates would not have to mention all the features given below in order to receive full credit. For example, in answering questions on character or style and period, giving two of the features listed would be sufficient. The supplied answers to questions on character give a list of features followed by two possible adjectives that describe the character of the piece. Candidates may equally well use a different adjective – the important thing is that they identify relevant musical features which support their personal response.

Marks are not awarded for individual tests but reflect the candidate's overall performance during the set of tests as a whole. Candidates are encouraged to use Italian or other musical terms in their answers where appropriate, and this is sometimes shown in the indicative responses below; any clear description is acceptable. The assessment criteria are given on page 3.

GRADE 4

Test 4C(i)

1. **E. German**
   Dynamics: Started p, cresc. to f in the middle, dim. to p towards the end
   Tempo: It stayed the same
   Tonality: Major
   Character: Repeated lilting rhythms, moderate tempo, major key; graceful, calm

2. **Reger**
   Dynamics: Sudden
   Articulation: Detached
   Tempo: It stayed the same
   Character: Mixture of staccato and legato notes, quite fast tempo, major key, mainly loud dynamic; lively, happy

3. **Gurlitt**
   Dynamics: Suddenly
   Articulation: Detached
   Tonality: Major
   Character: Strong/bold contrasts, fast tempo, major key; bright, lively

4. **Sigurbjörnsson**
   Dynamics: Mostly loud, but got quieter towards the end
   Articulation: Detached
   Tonality: Minor
   Character: Low pitch range, march-like rhythm, minor key, mainly loud dynamic; forceful/strong, solemn

5. **Villa-Lobos**
   Dynamics: Started mf, went a little quieter, ended f
   Tempo: It stayed the same
   Tonality: Major
   Character: Dance-like rhythms, simple tune, major key; lively, happy

6. **Grechaninov**
   Articulation: Detached
   Tempo: It slowed down twice – just after the middle and towards the end
   Tonality: Minor
   Character: Triple metre/strong downbeats, staccato accompaniment in the middle, minor key; dance-like, sad

7. **Stephen Duro**
   Dynamics: Quiet, got gradually louder, then quieter again towards the end
   Tempo: It stayed the same
   Tonality: Major
   Character: Jazzy rhythms, triple metre, 'catchy' tune, major key; happy, jaunty

8. **Steibelt**
   Dynamics: Started *p*, then *mf*, cresc. to *f*
   Articulation: Smooth
   Tonality: Minor
   Character: Minor key, moderate tempo, contrasts
   between quiet legato playing and louder staccato
   phrases; unsettled/changeable, serious

9. **Jensen**
   Dynamics: Sudden changes – moderately quiet, very
   quiet, fairly loud
   Articulation: First phrase staccato; last phrase legato
   Tonality: Major
   Character: Detached notes, fairly fast tempo, major key,
   dance-like rhythms; graceful, cheerful

10. **C. Franck**
    Dynamics: Started quietly, cresc. to *f* in middle, last
    phrase *pp*
    Tempo: It stayed the same
    Tonality: Minor
    Character: Smooth melody, slow tempo, minor key; sad,
    melancholic

Answers

GRADE 5

Test 5C(i)

1. Handel
   Articulation: Mostly detached/non-legato throughout
   Tonality: Major
   Character: Detached articulation, moderate tempo, major key, loud dynamic throughout; joyful, energetic/lively
   Style and Period: Baroque; strong melodic ideas (which are copied between the parts), use of a limited range of the keyboard, ornamentation, absence of dynamic change

2. Gershwin
   Dynamics: Gradual; at the end
   Tempo: It slowed down towards the end
   Tonality: Major
   Style and Period: 20th-century; jazzy style including 'bluesy' tune and chords, 'crushed notes', flexible rhythms

3. Grieg
   Dynamics: Started p, cresc. to f in the middle, dim. to pp at end
   Tempo: It slowed down twice – towards the middle and towards the end
   Character: Legato/cantabile melody, fairly slow tempo, major key; peaceful, lyrical
   Style and Period: Romantic; song-like melody, use of rubato, rich harmonies, use of sustaining pedal

4. Rameau
   Dynamics: Sudden; about a third of the way through
   Tempo: It slowed down towards the end
   Tonality: Minor
   Style and Period: Baroque; ornamentation, melodic ideas in both upper and lower parts, use of a limited range of the keyboard, light articulation

5. Mozart
   Dynamics: Second phrase much quieter
   Tempo: There was a rit./rall. towards the end
   Tonality: Major
   Style and Period: Classical; graceful melody with simple accompaniment, repeated ideas, clearly-defined phrases, gentle dynamic shaping

6. Falla
   Dynamics: ff, subito/suddenly p, back to ff at end
   Tempo: It stayed the same
   Character: Powerful/thick chords, strong dynamic and rhythmic contrasts, quite fast tempo; bold, vigorous
   Style and Period: 20th-century; strong repeated chords, wide dynamic range, use of accents, sudden changes, use of some dissonance, contrasts between major and minor

7. Christopher Norton
   Articulation: Smoothly
   Tonality: Major
   Character: Jazzy/syncopated rhythms, 'bluesy' tune with 'crushed notes', moderate/flowing tempo, major key; jaunty, 'happy-go-lucky'/light-hearted
   Style and Period: 20th-century; jazzy/syncopated rhythms, 'bluesy' melody and chords, call and response between top line and bass line

8. Lutosławski
   Dynamics: Around the middle; at the end
   Articulation: Detached
   Tempo: Back to original tempo, then accel. to the end
   Style and Period: 20th-century; dissonant/clashing notes, off-beat accents, changes of tempo, spiky articulation

9. Chopin
   Dynamics: Generally quiet throughout, gradual changes
   Articulation: Smoothly
   Character: Slow waltz tempo, minor key, step-wise melody in left-hand; sad, calm
   Style and Period: Romantic; cantabile melody, rich harmonies, use of sustaining pedal, flexible tempo/rubato

10. Kammel
    Dynamics: Louder; gradually
    Articulation: Detached
    Tempo: Rit./rall. towards the end
    Style and Period: Classical; clearly-defined, regular phrases with cresc. and dim., use of scale and arpeggio patterns, simple harmony